END YOUR YOUR RELATIONSH*T

WITH COMPASSION, SELF-RESPECT, AND LOGIC

A MEMOIR AND PRACTICAL GUIDE TO HELP YOU
END YOUR SH*TTY RELATIONSHIP

D.L. DEMPSEY

WRITERS REPUBLIC L.L.C.
515 Summit Ave. Unit R1
Union City, NJ 07087, USA

Website: *www.writersrepublic.com*
Hotline: *1-877-656-6838*
Email: *info@writersrepublic.com*

Ordering Information:
Quantity sales. Special discounts are available on quantity purchases by corporations, associations, and others. For details, contact the publisher at the address above.

Library of Congress Control Number: 2020937482
ISBN-13:   978-1-64620-336-9   [Paperback Edition]
                  978-1-64620-337-6   [Digital Edition]

Rev. date: 01/07/2021

END
YOUR
RELATIONSH*T

This book is dedicated to all of those who are alone in their relationships and feel they have no way out...

To those couples who know that it's over but stay for reasons they believe is out of their control...

To those who believe this unfulfilling life is all you have...

Let this book be your guide to greater things.

I believe in you.

Author D.L. Dempsey is not responsible for the outcomes during and after the break-up or divorce. This book is primarily intended for people who are in stale, stagnant, and unfulfilling relationships. Any physical abuse that occurs in your life needs to be reported to your law enforcement authorities for you to gain freedom.

Table of Contents

If you are in an exhausting, stagnant relationship and feel that you just need self-help books right now, this book may help <u>after</u> you've read books recommended by therapists that I've seen over the years such as:

<u>Codependent No More</u>: by Melody Beattie (with the workbook)

<u>Boundaries:</u> (Different version: Dating, Marriage, etc) by Dr. Henry Cloud & Dr. John Townsend

<u>The Five Love Languages:</u> by Gary Chapman

<u>Attached</u>: by Amir Levine

<u>I Hear You:</u> By Michael Sorensen

<u>Too Good to Leave, Too Bad To Stay:</u> *<u>A Step-by-Step Guide to Help You Decide Whether to Stay In or Get Out of Your Relationship:</u>* by Mira Kirshenbaum

Otherwise, read on if you're just ready to end it!

About the Author

D.L. Dempsey is a proud decorated military Veteran, a bad-ass single mom, and a first-time author. She wanted to give the world the book that she wished she had when she was stuck in a hamster wheel of a stale, unfulfilling, verbally and mentally-abusive relationship.

Though she is not a marriage/family therapist, she has most often been that person that people would go to for personal advice and guidance. She holds an Associate of Science in Public Health, a Bachelor's degree focused on conflict mediation and communication, a Master of Public Health, and a Master of Science in Nursing where she gained deep insight into human behavioral and psychiatric health.

Her Master's thesis focused on behaviors of women in substance abuse rehab in regard to relapse, the neurobiological changes that occur, and what kinds of problems can occur when people have histories of trauma. She still researches Adverse Childhood Experience Trauma studies and applies that concept to her practice as a Registered Nurse to this day.

Over the years she has provided a positive, life-changing impact on others' lives from helping family and old friends suffering abusive or unfulfilling marriages get through the barriers to starting and following through with their divorces. The advice and guidance she typically gives tends to start with thought-provoking questions that get to the root cause of the problem, then she may give options and resources that one can decide upon.

She has seen at least a dozen marriage and family therapists and chaplains over the last 9 years and will be sharing some of the most profound and useful tools that she has learned and successfully applied.

Acknowledgements

My mom. Through the process of ending the marriage and every moment ever since, I have felt her spirit watching over me and cheering me on. Rest in Peace forever and always.

My family, closest friends, and former mentors and bosses. You all have touched my life during its darkest times in your own special way. I am forever grateful for your compassion because you literally helped save my life.

My one and only son. You are my rock, my core, my purpose. I hope that as you grow, you continue seeing the silver linings in the darkness of the world while holding onto the realism of the challenges you'll face. I hope that you live a life full of purpose and service while remembering that I'll always cheer you on.

I owe a huge thank you to my best colleague Bill Thorton for taking the time to help me edit and do the parts of this process that I dreaded. You're amazing!!

Introduction

Hey you... you awesome, determined, and probably worn-out person reading this right now. This intro will explain some terms and concepts that you'll be seeing throughout this book. If you're anything like me, you might skip this so you can get to the meat and potatoes of the book. In this case, that is highly discouraged.

Here's a little bit about my story. I was 18 and a half, naive, didn't know how to set boundaries (or knew what they were), walked around with pretty heavy childhood baggage that I didn't know existed, and a guy - an acquaintance, 10 years older - came into my life right after I broke up with another older guy who had his own major problems. So yes, my ex was a rebound. Our first year of dating was pretty awesome. No complaints in that department (except having gained a lot of weight from feeling too comfortable around him), and after a year I felt good enough to move in with him. At that point, I started seeing more and more moments that to any experienced person would consider to be Red Flags, I just saw them as little challenges. As we got deeper into our relationship, I started seeing that he acted too strict and neurotic for my taste. A fork couldn't be left in the sink for that would make me a f*cking slob. I couldn't wear scoop-neck shirts in public because they drew too much attention, though those shirts were his favorite. Too many things. Perhaps you have your own list of Red Flags that you were blind to and stuck around without regard to them. I was too nice. I thought I could change him. I thought we could work through those things.

All I knew was his kind of man and didn't really know that other men existed. My stepdad was a manipulative closet pedophile. My mom worked a lot and was passive. My father was bipolar and was a closet meth-user to balance out his severe mood swings. My stepmom also worked a lot and just thought he was being himself because she knew how traumatic his childhood was. When I was 14, my virginity thief was a year older than my father, and was very manipulative and coercing. I hid it well out of fear of letting my family down, ruining my reputation, and the guy was nice to me because he told me all of the things every teenage girl wanted to hear - or so I thought. So what did I know? Did I know better? Nope.

Not really, this guy was nice. He drove 30 minutes to see me a few times, bought me ice cream, and didn't try to fuck me the first night we hung out. To me, at that time, he was the best man I had ever met because I didn't have many standards to compare him to. So, I stuck with him for the next 8 years.

It literally turned out like the old jump rope song, "someone and someone sitting in a tree... k-i-s-s-i-n-g. First comes love, then comes marriage, then comes a baby in a baby carriage". What else could have possibly been thrown into that easy 3-step process we learned so much about as kids?

I didn't even think about it, I just gave the only answer I knew: "yes". Immediately after, I envisioned celebrations, lots of sex, and that everything from here on out would be amazing considering that we would have a new, stable life together with my new job. I was leaving for Air Force Basic Training in 3 days so I knew that I was about to have a steady and stable income, free healthcare, and all of the other benefits that come with joining the military. Everything was going to be fresh, new, and amazing... so why not?

For the longest time I thought "Damn, does he just want my health benefits? Am I being used for my money? Does it piss him off that I make more money? Maybe that's all hurting his ego so he's projecting his anger onto me about all that? I was constantly second guessing our intentions of why we got married in the first place. Yes, he had insecurities and projected them onto me quite often, and I would in turn avoid him. Not healthy. He had narcissistic traits, then again I often wondered if he was just acting out the way he knows best because he never learned any better. I put my goals and ambitions before resolving those conflicts and having crucial discussions with him. I didn't even know where to start with those because I was never equipped with those skills. Over the next 7 years, it got to the point where I considered suicide more than once as a result of verbal abuse, but luckily and thankfully was strong enough to quickly overcome for the sake of my son. In other parts of my life I started trying to befriend and make amends with my enemies in a vicarious attempt to resolve my marriage issues.

This book is intended to help you learn how to end the relationship when you know deep down that it is already over. I wanted to leave him before shipping out to Basic Military Training, but I chose not to. I chose to get myself stuck in a pickle that I could have ended. Once I chose not to end it, every chance that I had after then, for 6 years, did not work out. I wasn't strong enough. Wasn't assertive enough. I took college courses on conflict resolution and mediation, and sought therapy on a weekly basis (with a mix of social workers, clinical psychologists, licensed marriage and family therapists, psychiatrists, and chaplains), and even avoided him by signing up for a bowling league (even though I knew I wasn't a good bowler).

I am sharing my experiences in a general sense because this is not a one-size-fits-all method. I want this book to benefit all people in all situations relating to shitty relationships in general. If you are with a narcissist, this whole process worked wonders with me because I learned how to control my own thoughts, feelings, and the divorce paperwork. I dissociated myself so far from any emotional attachment yet kept the whole process compassionate to him. I didn't give into his attempt to reel me back in and promise me the world, nor did any piece of me. Since the process focuses on compassion and making it as clean of a break as possible, it could certainly help many people in different situations.

I have to warn you: the tone I will be using throughout this book will be how I would talk to a close friend, so now please consider me to be that friend that you may have probably needed for quite some time.

Here's why.

I started this book by journaling to my past self from my present self, telling me what I should have done differently. Then, from both personal reflection and polls that I have conducted, it can take years of trial and error to find a quality therapist who really gets down to the core of your problems in the way that works for you. For me, I have sought care from 12 sources of therapy including mental health therapists, chaplains, psychologists, and social workers - and can only recall three who made a true impact on my life.

Throughout the book, you might see the newly-invented word, relationshi**t**. You might be wondering what exactly a relationshi**t** is. Just as it sounds, it is a relationship that is, well, shit. It just seems to flow so perfectly and sound so real and relatable that I figure it's a term I'll use from here on out.

A relationshi**p** should be two people that are independent, want to be together, and can mutually **relate** to one another on many levels - hence the root word "relation". They genuinely care for each other's emotional and spiritual well-being, they are compatible in many different ways, they know how to communicate, they are more than friends, and can depend on one another, etc. Among all of the other common traits that need to go into a quality relationship, we might as well call it a relationshi**t** when none of those are present.

This might sound cliche', but my life has been a trippy roller coaster ride. Except, it's been more of the kind of ride where my straps holding me in were made of the finest torn hand-me-down rags tied together... I'm grasping with my dear life a paper bag with baby animals in it... A cute fragile kitten by the name of Hope, a little duckling by the name of Dignity, and a little puppy with the name Peace.

With every curve and every loop I am frantically trying to grab Peace's ear and Dignity's tail while simultaneously clenching my butt cheeks hoping that the tied rags will not break... I'm shouting to my friends and family in the cars behind me to prepare to catch me if I do fall out, or if they catch one of my sweet baby animals to remind me they're there until I can recover and get them back. From hanging onto a shitty marriage/ relationshit for 8 years, I did end up losing peace, dignity, and hope there for a while... but I sure as hell found them after much trial and error and support from friends.

The last year of the marriage consisted of sleeping in separate rooms, taking our son to do things without the other parent, and found trends, triggers, and traps that made it easy for me to finally find that perfect time to leave.

Even years after that, I have known nearly a dozen people who have been in similar stagnant, hard to escape situations... Both men and women. Some common denominators that I found among those people were that they were either too nice, they would fear hurting the other person and would sacrifice their own well-being and happiness, or they were addicted to the status quo and feared change.

If one of those denominators sounds like something you might be going through, then please keep reading; I will be delving more into those common denominators later.

This book includes workbook-style pages where you will be highly encouraged to do some writing. Just how we learn the most fundamental skills in life, (ABCs, 123s), writing and reading/speaking it repeatedly will have more of a lasting impact than just a quick, passing thought.

I truly hope from the bottom of my heart that I can give you some tools to help you clear your head, get your life back, and live with purpose and fulfillment - alone.

If you find that this book is helpful, please share it with your friends that might be going through something as well. One thing I have learned is that I have friends who were in relationships that seemed perfectly fine from an outsider, but it wasn't until I started verbalizing things that helped me escape and start fresh that people started reaching out to me... telling me that their relationships were far from ideal and that they were stuck.

Having tools such as what I'm about to give you and sharing it with others is one small way that we are making this world a better, more tolerable, respectable and loving place.

Use this empty space to free-write any other thoughts you are having in this moment.

PART ONE.

Sometimes, removing our emotions about a situation can bring clarity to the root problems.

Someone very wise.

Chapter 1: Face the Facts
They're Right in Front of You, but
They Aren't Always Obvious.

There are plenty of relationship self-help books out there that try to help folks with: making that decision of whether to stay or go, how to make it work, how to recover from abuse, and so much more... but the purpose of this book is to help those people who are mutually in a relationship that is really already over, and no one knows how to get out.

These couples may have already talked about breaking up, but haven't.

They also may have cheated and found easy - yet unhealthy - ways out of the relationships, and still remain stuck.

This is the book meant for those couples, with the intent of helping guide them through the process of self-reflection and taking the initiative to break up with empathy and compassion with as few hard feelings left behind as possible.

The anecdotes shared are all true stories, and I do lack a filter, so you have been warned.

Now I am not a mind reader, and I don't know if you and I have ever met. But I will tell you this... If you pick up this book, you are likely here because:

- A: You are in a relationship that you no longer want to be in
- B: You are in a relationship that you are not sure if you want to still be in

- C: You are in a relationship that you never really thought you would feel so damn bored or lonely in...

If one of those is at least somewhat close, then you may fall into one of more of these categories:

- You avoid each other, and occasionally cheat.
- You're addicted to the status quo and fear change.
- You worry about others' perception of you, such that they may think you are selfish for leaving the other person.
- You have a tendency to be codependent on a subconscious level. You tend to allow your partner's perceived happiness dictate your own intrinsic happiness.
- You're optimistic that things will turn around for the better, even if you have tried for years to make that happen.
- You realize that your relationship is harder than it seemed, and you may value yourself highly by your willingness to not give up what you've worked so hard for.

Among many authors I discovered in my research, a Doctor of Psychology named Beverly D. Flaxington, explains in her articles how a main problem that couples tend to face with being stuck in a relationship that they cannot get out of, has a lot to do with insecurity. The insecurity tends to involve one's own level of confidence and the reliance of the partner to maintain the other's self-worth and value.

For example, this can be compared to a man valuing himself by how he can successfully give a female an orgasm. Though her ability to orgasm may not even be related to the man's abilities, he may still feel his ego become crushed regardless if it was his ability or not. He may then seek out other women to "value himself" with, or he may avoid further attempts and take his anger and embarrassment out on the partner in subtle or unrelated ways.

Another example is when a partner has friends of the opposite sex and they hug, or sit next to one another, or even have conversation. The insecurity will blind the partner and throw him/her into a state of possessiveness and fear, causing unprecedented - or in many cases - expected and unfortunate immature and annoying behaviors because of an underlying anxiety.

She explains that another common factor is the fear of being alone. Sometimes couples that have been together for numerous years don't know any other life other than what their comfort zone is. Even if it's an abusive, toxic, or plain old boring relationship, that fear of being alone is far scarier than anything you might already be going through.

Now let's talk about codependency for a brief moment. Codependency is defined by Merriam-Webster as, "a psychological condition or a relationship in which a person is controlled or manipulated by another who is affected by a pathological condition." The last part made me wonder, What if this person has an undiagnosed pathological condition? What if this person claims to have nothing wrong and will never even try to seek help? I found that when in doubt, pretend as if the other does have something pathological going on in order to keep you safe. It's the same idea of disease prevention. If someone acts like they might have the Coronavirus when they chalk it up to the common cold, you're better off keeping your distance.

Co-dependency is broadly defined as the dependence on the needs or control of another person; in other words, you put your partner's needs first at the detriment of your own. If you are risking your intrinsic joy and happiness to make the partner happy, then you may be suffering through codependency - and that is a serious problem. This concept can be blatantly obvious from a third person perspective, or it may be hidden under the facade of a quality relationship you may have been portraying for so long. The following tips were discovered through therapy.

Here are some examples of codependent behavior:

1. You "walk on eggshells" to either: avoid upsetting your partner or to ensure there is constant peace. This is where you base any decision you make on the possible response from the other person. You are probably codependent to your partner.

2. You get energized and addicted to the adrenaline rush when you two may fight or argue. That adrenaline rush may be a subconscious "high" that you end up craving, so you may either contribute to perpetuating an argument, initiating one, or even cheat or act in a way that

may potentially spark a fight. You are probably codependent to the rush you feel.

3. Maybe you are addicted to your current status and state of mind, and if you change anything then you may become stressed out. You are probably codependent to the status quo.

Now, **why have you been staying?** Many reasons may pop into your head... write them down without even thinking about them. Don't second guess yourself. Don't worry about your partner finding this book. Don't worry about a damn thing, just for a moment. Just free-write.

_____
_____
_____
_____
_____

Look at what you just wrote. Read it out loud two times. Now ask yourself if those are worth suffering for and worth being lonely for.

Are they?

Now, ask yourself these questions **verbatim** and don't filter your thoughts. Say and/or write the first thoughts that come to mind.

1. Do any of these ideas suggest I may be codependent?

2. Do these reasons bring me joy?

3. What is good about staying?

4. What is **not** so good about staying?

5. What do I truly want? (*"I don't know" doesn't count.* Single words don't count. Be detailed.)

<u>The Game-Changer from my Thera-py Experience:</u> **The Thinking Traps**

The one tool that I found to be the greatest, most practical, and easily accessible is the awareness of Cognitive Distortions, also known as the Thinking Traps. This is a tool that I use even still to this day. Not even kidding. It was tweaked and implemented into general cognitive therapeutic practice by Dr. David D. Burns, who is literally my hero for having created such a mind-clearing medicine.

The Thinking Traps truly changed my complete way of thinking from my many years of therapy and practice using it. It's a cognitive thinking exercise that helps us realize the facts behind the types of thoughts we might have.

Once we are able to establish the type of trap, what thoughts or actions that get us trapped, and what triggers the trap to close, then we become transcended into a state of consciousness that makes us feel in control of ourselves, our wandering minds, and our volatile emotions.

The Unhealthy Thinking **Traps**

1. **All-or-Nothing, Black and White. Thinking that one thing always leads to another.** *If I am not perfect, I am a failure.*

2. **Over-Generalizing. Seeing patterns based on a single event or person.** *All men/women are the same.*

3. **Negative Filter. You tend to focus on only the negative.** *I only see what fails and cannot see the successes.*

4. **Discounting Positives. Anything good that happens is not good enough.** *That good thing doesn't count, or isn't realistic.*

5. **Jumping to Conclusions. Mind-reading and fortune-telling.** *I know what the other is thinking, or I will never find happiness.*

6. **Catastrophic or Minimized Thinking. Blowing situations out of proportion or making them less important.** *My thoughts don't matter if I can't win an argument. All of this makes me want to just end my life.*

7. **Emotional Reasoning. Assuming that your emotions depict the facts.** *I feel sad or upset so I must be the negative one in this relationship.*

8. **Should/Must/Ought thinking. These are where unspoken expectations occur, therefore leading to frustration and disappointment.** *She*

should know what I expect. I must not argue to avoid upsetting him.

9. **Labels. Where we assign labels to ourselves or others.** *I'm an idiot, he's an asshole, she's useless.*

10. **Personalization. Blaming ourselves for something that isn't our fault.** *He's angry because of me, I deserve this.*

If you sit and think about your emotions regarding your partner and your relationshit, make a list of them and see if you can place a thinking trap on each. If you do identify some traps, think about alternative, healthy ways of thinking. You can literally do this every time you feel confused, frustrated, or upset to hep you see your own mind in a more logical way.

Here is one example:

My Problem: "**He thinks** I'm a **failure** as a wife because I am **always** a slob, and calls me out for **everything** that I do around the house. It makes me feel like **I can't win** and that I **should just run away**".

<u>My Thinking Traps:</u>
    "I'm a failure", "slob" = labeling
    "always", "everything..." = overgeneralizing
    "I can't win" = personalization, all-or-nothing
    "Should just run away" = should-thinking.
    "He thinks" = mind-reading

INSTEAD, I could say: "We fight about the cleanliness of our house and he is most often the one to initiate blame. It makes me feel defeated and I need a healthy way to cope and overcome".

Read those two examples back to back. See the difference? Less emotion, more clarity. Give it a try!

Another example: She hasn't texted me back. **I must** text her too much and come off as **clingy**. **Maybe I should** stop altogether.

<u>My Thinking Traps:</u>
    " I must..." = Jumping to conclusions.
    "Clingy" = labeling
    "Should" = Should thinking/false expectations

INSTEAD, I could say: She hasn't texted me back. I hope everything is okay. To stop myself from freaking out, I will give her two more days to respond before I check in.

I am convinced that every person on this planet falls into these thinking traps on a regular basis. They are so easy to stumble across, but doing this exercise and seeing how many traps you can dig your way out of in your mind will help you create a map of all landmines and booby traps before you victimize yourself again.

Your problem:

_____
_____
_____
_____

Your Thinking Traps:

_____
_____
_____
_____

Your NEW way of wording your problem:

_____
_____
_____
_____

How was that for you?

I encourage you to take some extra time and try this exercise everytime you feel that you've been caught in a thinking trap. You can do this in a journal, on a notepad app, or on sticky notes. Whatever you prefer! I did this every day for 6 weeks and it changed my life.

You've tried everything... now what?

You may have tried doing the Five Love Languages together, you may have even done it yourself and tried estimating your partners love languages... you may have done different personality tests, therapy sessions, long night talking, gone to friends for advice, and you may have even tried self-medicating in some way.

You may have tried literally everything and now you are at the point where you know nothing else will work, your partner won't change, and even your partner might know it's over...

Now one of you has to take the initiative to make a move.

Now I must be clear, in no way am I shaming the above sources. They could be used as fantastic and reliable guides to help you figure out that maybe this life is not the life for you. You are here because you already learned that and you are ready to make your move.

When I went through my divorce, which was about a 2 - year long process, I did all of those things. The Five Love Languages, all those videos and personality tests, self-therapy, marriage counseling, self-help books...

They were all amazing resources and guided me to realize the reality and severity of my situation. Now you are in this sad, sad reality and I want you to take my figurative hand as I pull you out of this toilet bowl of a life. This is the book I wish I had.

Chapter 2:
The Sly Signs and the Wise Whys

The Sly Signs
The Wise "Whys"
The Mirror of My Childhood

The Sly Signs

Whether you believe in the universe, the seasons, astrology, horoscopes, God, Karma, Allah, Buddha, or any higher being greater than yourself, know that they are real and they are watching out for you. They will show you sly, subtle signs that you may or may not acknowledge or notice. If you do, I encourage you to follow those signs. Here's a story about one of my signs, marking a major turning point in my life.

In the final year of my marriage, there were some times when I thought it was the right moment... The right moment to file for divorce, leave him, to end it all, and to start my life over yet none of them ever sat well with me. I did not believe that things would have worked out in my favor.

The most significant moment that I can remember is after we had one of our regularly scheduled big fights, I gave my husband the best mic-dropping, heartfelt, improvised, powerful speech of my entire life about how toxic we were and how we would be better off as single parents. I was even surprised when he replied that I made a very good point and that he understands when typically he would fight back.

Not five minutes later, I started vomiting in the kitchen sink. I've never thrown up in my entire adult life (without alcohol involved), and low and behold I was surprisingly pregnant again. I took my birth control pill religiously, and we did not have sex often.

The next 24 hours I couldn't hardly speak because I was in such shock about the situation. Now why would the universe give us another child to fight in front of, to show how to survive being verbally and mentally fucked with, or how to be a bully? Why would that happen, and why now?

That whole week we kept talking about how long we're going to wait to tell people, and because her last child was super healthy with no problems, we decided to tell everyone right away. People were surprised, especially my closer friends that knew we were having problems. They were a little concerned.

The optimistic side of me started thinking that maybe this is a second chance. Maybe things will get better, maybe we will be amazing parents having two kids, maybe this baby is a miracle and that the universe is telling us that we shouldn't split up. Maybe the universe is trying to tell us that things will improve and maybe... Shit, who was I kidding? I was still quite pessimistic that things will get better. My optimism during that week was forced by this wonderful surprise. I didn't want a baby to grow inside of me while I survived day to day with a depressive state of mind.

Eight days later, I woke up with a puddle of blood in bed. We had plans to go on a trip that weekend to help save the marriage (which I was actually dreading), but I ended up going straight to the hospital instead.

While lying in the ER bed, I felt stuck... stuck on why this happened, why the timing, what what the purpose? Was somebody in the afterlife looking out for me? Was it a blessing in disguise? My mind was

flooded with all of these reasons and explanations...
Which made me wonder about that whole life
philosophy that everything happens for a reason... Or is
it that something happens and we find every possible
reason to make us feel better about it?

The way I see it is, that the universe, God,
guardian angels, whoever is out there was trying to tell
me that it wasn't the right time to leave him yet.

At that point in my life, I had just been promoted
to Staff Sergeant, my Air Force enlistment was coming
to an end in seven months, and I was waiting on my
nursing school applications. I had some major life
changes coming my way and this miscarriage felt like
a tsunami of mixed emotions... regret for having told
people so soon, resilient enough to not hold onto the
fact that I just lost an embryo, curiosity about why this
happened, and most of all - gratitude for the realization
that I needed to change my priorities.

Then came the shame and self doubt... perhaps
the next stage of the grief process, depression.

Did I lose the baby because I didn't love myself
anymore? I mean, all of the times when I would get in
my car and angrily drive away after being exhausted
from trying to stand up for myself during a verbally
abusive fight, thinking that I should start planning my
funeral now then swerve into traffic... is that why I lost
the baby? Because if I can't take care of my own mental
health, how could I care for another baby?

Did I lose it because I didn't love my husband anymore and feared I could never love someone new the way they deserve to be loved?

Did I lose the baby because I already shared all of my love and purpose in life for my soon-to-be 2 year old boy and had no room for more?

None of that mattered anymore. I had to be in the moment and realize that this was meant to be. It was a sign that I had to slow down.

I was so ready to just drop the ball and divorce him right then and there, but with all these changes coming up in the next six months I probably would have made a huge mistake by ending it too soon.

A month later I took a solo, unplanned, spontaneous trip to Lake Tahoe (my most local happy place) then started keeping tabs on all of the signs pointing me in the right direction. I got accepted to Nursing school - a life goal accomplished. Then I filed for divorce and ended my military career. It all happened at once, so fast, and it was the absolute best decision I could've ever made. Had I started making changes sooner, my mindset may have been different, more stressed, and everything may not have worked out the way it did.

Take a moment to think about some signs you may have observed recently that made you think that your situation is not what you should be living with. Find at least one before continuing on.

The Wise "Whys"

For 6 years I researched why people stay in such shitty conditions, mainly to help me understand why I was staying in mine. I wanted to know why people CHOOSE to stay in the driver's seat of a car with flat tires and no more gas. What is it about human behavior that leads us to forget any measure of confidence that allows self-loathing or living in a situation that does not cater positively to your mental, emotional, spiritual, and physical well-being?

As I learned about attachment styles in therapy, I started to realize all the reasons why I was staying for so long. It turned out that I was able to use those specific reasons as individual goals to work on and that there are many types of therapeutic treatments and books on each.

There are infinite unique cases out there that you might not relate to, yet there are many that you may. Some of the following reasons why you may have been stuck for so long may resonate with you and help you realize that you are not alone in this world.

1. **"Silver linings" perception** - You are seeing a negative relationship in a positive light, creating a false sense of optimism that change will come and that everything will "be okay".

2. **Low self esteem** - Not realizing that you are way more valuable than what you allow yourself to be perceived as. You don't set clear boundaries for yourself, and may not have learned how to in the past.

3. **Avoidance coping** - Avoiding the partner
    prevents conflict, is more simple, and is an easy
    habit to form. Avoiding the partner can be seen
    as the easy way to continue living your day
    to day life without taking the initiative to find
    enough courage to do what you need to do.

4. **Toxic Empathy** - One person understands why
    the other is the way he/she is and tolerates the
    partner's toxic behaviors as a result. This is
    a common factor primarily in narcissistically-
    abusive relationships.

5. **Codependency** - Making the partner's esteem
    and pleasure a priority over your own, and/
    or taking the responsibility for your partner's
    problems. This may have been learned in
    those raised by abusive or substance-addicted
    households.

6. **Unwillingness to hurt the other and/or the
    kids** - You're a kind person who doesn't want
    to hurt anyone. You're just too nice. Maybe
    continuing the never-ending fight to make
    things right will teach yourself (and the kids - if
    applicable) that hard work, dedication, and many
    years of misery is worth a divorce/breakup 20
    years down the road.

7. **Fear of change -** You are addicted to the
    status quo. The idea of having new stress from
    adjusting to a new life, financial changes, let
    alone the confrontation of ending it - seem far
    worse than what you're used to.

8. **Fear of dating** - Your expectations may be higher out of fear of history repeating itself, dates' expectations may not line up with yours, unspoken expectations are tricky and even more stressful.

9. **Fear of being alone** - Even if in the presence of a partner with whom you cannot relate to nor get along with, it seems better than not being around anyone at all.

10. **Believing that this is normal** - You may have grown up with parents who fought a lot, maybe they were abusive towards one another or toward you, maybe your parents were in abusive households growing up and transmitted their historical trauma in subtle ways, had substance abuse disorders, or raised you to think that if a boy/girl is picking on you then that means they like you.

When we believe in a certain outcome based on the sole possibility of that outcome, we are living with Limiting Beliefs. They're the devil. Holding ourselves to those nasty limiting beliefs (such as "This is normal", "I am nothing without my partner", "Life will suck if we end it", "Change is scary and I will not succeed", or even "Ending it will hurt the kids"...) will create a facade of a life based on a 'What-if' perception.

Your decisions, if based on those limiting beliefs, will forever remain as the diseases that prevent your life from thriving and being what you deserve. It will be painful and difficult regardless if you stay or try to leave, but think about the long-term benefit of each.

If you were to become diagnosed with a disease that gives you a short prognosis, would you just go with it and allow yourself to suffer? Or, would you take advice from a survivor on how to take control of the disease before it controls you?

Please know that you **can** help yourself. You **can** control your beliefs. You are allowed to take a break from relying on your higher power and take your life into your own hands.

I did, and I finally was able to learn and love myself for who I am and keep my distance from those who do not.

The Mirror of My Childhood

Dr. Nadine Burke Harris' brilliant concept of Adverse Childhood Experiences and their effects on physical health hold true, especially if you find yourself stuck in a relationship that mimics your parents' relationship when you were young. Some examples that I have may trigger intense emotions, so please read on with caution while making sure you're in a safe spot, away from any traps such as alcohol or drugs, and are ready to figure yourself out.

Examples of childhood traumas that you may have subconsciously been repeatedly exposed to in your relationshit.

1. You want your parent's attention, yet they just look at their phone/tv/anything that is not you. They did not engage with the love that you needed, possibly similar to your partner.

2. Your parents rewarded you with presents and spoiled you, regardless of how they may have manipulated you with them to get you to do what they wanted. Your partner in this case might spoil you with gifts and use them against you.

3. You may have had parents with alcohol, drugs, or other substance addictions, so you felt like you needed to fend for yourself. In your relationship, you may feel that you too need to fend for yourself if your partner is (or is not) addicted to any substances. You're just doing what you're used to doing.

4. You may have had parents that did not listen
    to you if you needed to tell them something is
    important, yet you had to live with them anyway.
    In your relationshit, you may have a partner
    who doesn't listen and pushes problems under
    the rug.

5. Your parents may have just simply tolerated one
    another and did not actively show their love. You
    may be used to that type of relationship and feel
    that you have no way out because that's all you
    know.

Perhaps you see where I'm getting at; we might be staying because we're experiencing something that we've been used to our whole lives. Maybe what we're going through mirrors what we were exposed to as children. Though that's not always the case, I definitely can relate and know many people who can too.

Take a moment to write about how your parents' relationship was, if you can remember... even if you had single parents, foster parents, you name it. This is your personal development we're talking about.

_____
_____
_____
_____
_____
_____

Your current relationship may be affecting you physically just as it is mentally, yet if you were exposed to similar relationships from your parents and guardians during childhood, this physical and psychological dilemma may have started at an early age.

It is NOT too late, in fact right now is the perfect time to change that. It took me 27 years. From therapy and friends who knew my ex and parents, I saw sign after sign that I married my father in many ways and was in the same boat my mom was.

Chapter 3:
Why We Might End Up Here

*The Media &
Personal Boundary Abuse Disorder*

Entertainment and Media.

Growing up, we have all listened to music and seen shows and movies, plays, etc. with some sort of romantic plot or theme. After years of being repeatedly exposed to similar themes regarding love, all of the false romantic convictions that Hollywood, the music industry, Broadway, etc. convey become deeply engraved in the subconscious.

Like a toxic oil that coats our lenses that allow us to see the world around us, Hollywood and the music industry has misguided our romantic perceptions, our ability to see reality, and our willingness to make educated decisions.

1. Myth: Men should spill their hearts and go above and beyond to impress a woman with grand gestures early in a relationship.

   Reality: On one hand, grand gestures do not work for everyone. On the other hand, grand gestures may allow for your partner's disappointment because they may eventually start expecting more.

2. Myth: Love at first sight means true love forever.

   Reality: Our brains get a rush of dopamine (the feel-good neurotransmitter), and makes us crave that rush. Then we seek every avenue possible to get a "hit" of that rush, therefore causing an addiction-like behavior about another person. We might sacrifice our own happiness, basic needs, and common sense to simply feel that rush, then realize it may have all been a waste of time... As if that candy bar was not as good tasting as it looked and how I fantasized about. Now if a relationship does flourish from that initial lust, then they are most likely to claim that it was love from the start.

3. Myth: There's one and only person for you, aka "The One".

    Reality: Researchers such as Clinical Psychologist Craig Malkin support the finding that people who believe there is only one person for them, they tend to flee the relationship when issues start to arise because they did not expect anything but an easy, effortless time together.

4. Myth: Women feel they need to be saved or be swept off their feet by an attractive man to be happy.

    Reality: Disney Princess movies have engraved the idea that women need to be saved by men. In reality, there are women who feel they need to be saved but also may have self esteem issues, may tend to become codependent and rely too much on the man, and may not know if the man has ulterior motives. Get to know the man before giving him your life just as gratitude for his service to you.

5. Myth: Opposites Attract

    Reality: Movies such as Titanic, Pretty Woman, and Cinderella convey this notion that two people with drastic socioeconomic disparities are brought up with different views of the world, different daily routines, and very different values. Not that love is not possible, it would be increasingly difficult to relate to one another on a day to day basis, and therefore be a trigger for arguments. Personality speaking, opposite personalities are easy to clash, so it is crucial that each person tailor their communication styles to speak the language of the other. If one was raised by abusive parents, one may have trouble with bottling up emotions and hiding from conflict versus someone who was raised with stability, confidence, and high standards.

6. Myth: That "Honeymoon feeling" lasts forever.

   Reality: Movies that portray a couple living "happily ever after" at the end of many movies ends it at the best, most exciting part. All of the challenges, trial and error, and character- building situations that create a happily ever after are omitted.

   Such endings convey the idea that once all of the trials and tribulations that a couple endures just to be together end up being the only challenges they have to face. I like to compare those endings to a race... any type of race really. You race, you struggle, you win, and you celebrate and move forward with your life. It sets up some unrealistic expectations that even I have fallen brainwashed to.

   In reality, I compare it to a race where the finish line is at the edge of the ocean line. You race, you struggle, you win, you celebrate, then adapt to the change in environment, struggle some more, you swim, you sink, you may or may not get saved, you float and tread water for years, then depending on how everything for the individual works out, you might find land again and then have to endure other dangers and obstacles.

Movies with unrealistic romance are notorious for preying on our neurobiological makeup, triggering our brains' emotional systems to manifest certain emotions, releasing rushes of dopamine that make us craving more. We then might tend to try and live vicariously through the movies by increasing our romantic expectations to the real world. Many people tend to watch romantic comedies after a bad break-up or while obsessing or fantasizing about a crush, but why? Perhaps we dig ourselves into the hole of romantic movies to try and reverse the intense intimate emotions that take over our minds by seeing the actors endure what we try to avoid.

There have been too many times in my life where I would watch movies like Friends With Benefits, The Ugly Truth, or any Adam Sandler-Drew Barrymore movie while thinking of my crush. I'd imagine trying moves and lines from the movie with my love interest, hoping that he would react the way the guy did in the movie. I would play out an entire scene as if my crush and I were the actors. Now why would I expect him to react the same way? Would it have something to do with these movies being the only healthy relationships I've been exposed to? Or would it have something to do with my increased levels of dopamine making me want more of what I saw, so I can apply it to my own life so I can take a bigger hit of that rush than what the movie provided?

Daring to set boundaries is about having the courage to love ourselves, even when we risk disappointing others.

- *Brene Brown*

Personal Boundary-Abuse Disorder

One month after I gained the courage of a lifetime and had my ex served with divorce papers, I dove straight into an intense two-year Master of Science in Nursing program. I heavily researched the topic of drug abuse rehabilitation for women for my Master's thesis project and found **several** similar themes in drug dependency that related to my marriage. In the midst of learning much about these women, I had this overwhelming realization that they had many of the same triggers, historical events, and levels of self sufficiency that I did while stuck in my poor relationship.

Although "Personal Boundary-Abuse Disorder" is not an official mental health diagnosis, it is a theoretical, metaphorical disorder that I felt would slap an adequate label on my life to help it make some more sense.

My definition of Personal Boundary Abuse Disorder:

A chronic disorder in which a person has difficulty setting one's own boundaries and allowing safe, reasonable, and acceptable behaviors from others and establishing healthy ways of responding to such contradicted behaviors. People with this disorder may have the ability to successfully end a relationship, friendship, or acquaintanceship with one who crosses such boundaries yet ends up in the same situation repeatedly.

People with this theoretical disorder may have had boundary issues in one's family while growing up, or may have never learned how to speak up when uncomfortable.

You have the right to your personal boundaries. If you are uncomfortable being with someone, physically or emotionally checked-out, or just plain unhappy, **you have the right to get out and get on with your life. You are not stuck. You are not choosing to stay stuck. You simply need to think differently.**

Now to compare this to Substance Abuse Disorder:

The Substance Abuse and Mental Health Services Administration, a branch of the US Department of Human and Health Services, defines Substance Abuse Disorder as, "*Substance use disorders occur when the recurrent use of alcohol and/or drugs causes clinically significant impairment, including health problems, disability, and failure to meet major responsibilities at work, school, or home*".

Specific criteria of the disorder include:

1. Craving the drug
2. Wanting to cut down but unable to
3. Taking the substance in larger amounts for longer periods of time
4. Neglecting other main parts of your life for the use of said substance

5. Continuing to use even if it becomes a problem in your personal life, physical, or mental health
6. Using substances in situations that put you in danger
7. Needing more to get the level of effect you want
8. Withdrawal symptoms relieved by taking more of the substance

How do they compare?

The Substance Abuse	The Self - Boundary Abuse
Craving the drug →	Craving a certain type of attention from your partner
Wanting to cut down but unable to →	You want out but feel stuck, unable to initiate confrontation
Taking the substance in larger amounts for longer periods of time →	You tolerate or put-up with your problems, they may intensify, and are unresolved
Neglecting other main parts of your life for the use of said substance →	You avoid/cancel plans with friends/ family to stay with the partner, emotions might trigger you at work, maybe you only do what your partner wants
Continuing to use even if it becomes a problem in your personal life, physical/mental health →	You may have lost some friends & sacrificed important pieces of you to try & save your relationship
Using substances in situations that put you in danger →	You stay even if it gives you anxiety/ depression or if you fight regularly

Needing more to get the level of effect you want →	Needing attention from your partner to get the self esteem, false pleasure, and faux joy that you so desire
Withdrawal symptoms relieved by taking more of the substance →	You two might fight then the partner will reel you back in and make you feel "safe"

Take a moment to ponder this. Substance Abuse disorder contains a wide array of different substances and their varying effects on individual people, yet overall there are many similarities all manifested in customized ways - different people, different situations, different drugs. Substance abuse disorders can even have associative effects, or the 'second-hand' effect - causing loss of trust, interest, and discomfort in those who might feel that your dependency takes priority.

The relationship between one staying stuck in a chemical dependency and another in a poor relationship encompasses the concept of codependency. Not everyone in long term shitty relationships are necessarily codependent, but consider it to be a main underlying issue if you meet some of the criteria in the chart above.

When I read the book Codependent No More by Melody Beattie, I gained insight as to how a major relationship between one who takes care of an alcoholic family member and loses oneself in the process can be similar to the potential outcomes of one who puts in all efforts into sustaining a hopeless relationship.

Comparing the struggles that the alcoholic family member, the caregiver, and what I endured made me realize that substance abuse and personal boundary abuse go hand in hand in a sort of toxic mindset of a twisted puppeteer. Part two will walk you through the cognitive mindset changes that I learned in therapy, and I hope that you take the time to participate.

The most world-renowned method of recovering from substance abuse disorders is the 12 Steps of Alcoholics Anonymous.

The 12 Steps of People-Pleasers Anonymous

As you learned about the comparison between abusing substances to abusing your boundaries, I hope that you may have had at least one little epiphany. You may be excellent at setting boundaries in general, yet if you have been stuck for so long in this situation you may be lacking the technique because of emotional attachments. You may be in a mentally and emotionally abusive relationshit, and if you are, then this is super important. If you both are mentally checked-out but are not in an abusive situation, this can work for you taking control over your own mind and areas of improvement. If you are doubting any of it, focus on that. Nurture that doubt. Ask yourself what exactly you're doubting and if it's worth looking into. It could be the lottery ticket that you doubted you'd win.

The 12 steps coming up is directly from Alcoholics Anonymous, and some parts are rephrased to fit this kind of situation, as shown in [brackets]. FYI - I left the following 12 steps in second-person, so when you read "we this" and "we that", think of it as you going through this enlightenment with everyone else reading this book and going through something similar to what you are. You are definitely not alone in this. So let's put our drinks down and think about the 12 steps and how they can be applied to your almost-new life.

Step 1: We admitted we were powerless over [our past traumas, our current problems, and our triggers] — that our lives had become unmanageable.

* Think about all of the times that your lines have been crossed, all of the times you went out of your way to

accommodate the other person while you were still unhappy, and even as far back into your childhood that you can remember. Are you a people pleaser? Do you try keeping the peace by holding your tongue? Are there moments from your early childhood where you had to do that, and now you have issues with setting boundaries? Admitting is the first step before moving to Step 2. If you don't admit your problems, the rest of the staircase will crumble. *

Step 2: Came to believe that a Power greater than ourselves could restore us to sanity.

* If you already believe in a greater Power, then this is the time to either enhance your practice in restoring your faith or seek counseling through your services. If you are atheist or agnostic, this is where things get tricky. I have been agnostic for the longest time yet I always believed in karma, balance (yin yang), and that everything happens for a reason. Take some time to think about what motivates you to live by your true values. If you question your values, then you should stay on Step 2 until you get clarity on that. Start reading some self-help books like _Think Like a Monk_ by Jay Shetty or _Whole Again_ by Jackson MacKenzie. Find your values and enhance your faith in any kind of greater Power before you try Step 3. This is essential. *

Step 3: Made a decision to turn our will and our lives over to the care of [my higher power] _as we understood [our higher power]_.

* Think of this as where you surrender, quit, and make yourself believe that something greater than what you have now can save your life. Here, you mentally jump your sinking ship into frightening, potentially life-changing and rejuvenating waters. Many in Step 3 see

*this step as the greatest challenge you'll face: Going cold-turkey on everything that you are currently doing and telling your higher power that you yourself do not know what's best for you in this moment. So now you're leaving it in your higher Power's hands. As we spoke about earlier in this book about the Sly Signs and Wise Whys, those signs and whys could very well be more clear and up-front once you take this step. ***

Step 4: Made a searching and fearless moral inventory of ourselves. (writing assignment)

** The 3 main areas of inventory you should take note of are: **Resentment, fear, and childhood traumas.** What do you resent? Make a list of all of the things, situations, people, behaviors, etc that piss you off, and try to realize the power those resentments have over you. You might not really know where all of it comes from, but you have to write them out and just let the thoughts flow. Then think to yourself... out of all of those, what have you also projected onto others? What are valid, and could you have coped with them in a better way? Did you experience any resentments in your childhood against any adults or other kids? Being able to give yourself the power to open up about this kind of information will help you find your improvement areas and make sense out of why everything has happened the way they have. Do the same with all of your fears. Think about a fear that you have in the moment then ask yourself, 'What are you really afraid of?' Think of an answer, write it down, then ask yourself again, 'What are you really afraid of?' Again, think back to your childhood and what those moments meant for you. All of this information that you are digging up from your core might cause physical symptoms in your gut, chest, and head. So when you feel those, meditate on them and focus on healing those*

thoughts. Write them all down so you won't need to store them in your mind anymore and it'll act as a guide for Step 5. This can take several days for you to finish.*

Step 5: Admitted to Your Higher Power, to ourselves, and to another human being the exact nature of our wrongs. (Verbal assignment)

*This is where you take ownership of everything that you discovered in Step 4. This is where you verbally tell someone that cares about you, even if it's only your higher Power. It can be the most powerful, anxiety-ridden, gut-wrenching, vulnerable moment you might feel. It's where you take responsibility for your side of your situation, for you are not strictly a victim. It does not discount any times when you may have been made a victim, yet some behaviors and thoughts may have gotten you into those situations to begin with. This is where you might feel the first major feeling of relief, letting out all of the troubles from your past that have been subconsciously haunting you. *

Step 6: Were entirely ready to have [your higher Power] remove all these defects of character.

* Now that you've written down and spoken your moral inventory, close your eyes, take a deep belly-breath, and exhale. You have now made for your higher power a clearly-defined list of your core reasons why your life has ended up where it is, which gives your higher power a guide on how to fix you. It's like you literally just created an instruction manual for yourself! That's HUGE! *

Step 7: Humbly asked Your Higher Power to remove our shortcomings.

* Verbally ask your higher power to remove everything you listed out. This releases your responsibility for those and lifts a heavy weight off of you. *

Step 8: Made a list of all persons we had harmed, and became willing to make amends to them all.

* You may have lost contact with people, close friends, family members, or even friendly acquaintances because you may have put your relationship first. If you think back to Step 4 and how you may have projected your own resentments onto others, you might realize that you should make amends with those people. *

Step 9: Made direct amends to such people wherever possible, except when to do so would injure them or others.

* Make the amends that you need to but do not sacrifice your or their personal safety for it.*

Step 10: Continued to take personal inventory and when we were wrong, promptly admitted it.

* This is a lifelong practice. Once you continue taking note of your resentments, fears, and other struggles, nurture them as you have and admit it right away. Master this skill! This is where sustainability and accountability happens. *

Step 11: Sought through prayer and meditation to improve our conscious contact with [my higher Power] as we understood [my higher Power], praying only for knowledge of [my power's] will for us and the power to carry that out.

*This is where you admit that you have been actively seeking clarity and understanding in the high power that you chose. You meditate and seek guidance on your inventory items. You are accountable and are doing your best. ***

Step 12: Having had a spiritual awakening as the result of these steps, we tried to carry this message to [other people stuck in poor relationships], and to practice these principles in all our affairs.

*This is where you pay it forward, take the lessons you learned, and help someone else. You can take everything you learned and even apply it to all areas of life, not just alcohol and boundary-less relationships. ***

PART TWO.

The Preparation.
Figure you out.

Now, let's figure **you** out.

This exercise may take some time and intrinsic exploration, so bookmark this next page and return to it later if you need.

Close your eyes and think about specifics in your relationshit that reinforce that you two are done.

Think back to the most recent or greatest magnitude argument/fight, or a moment where everything changed how you view your partner, or anything that jumps out at you. Briefly write about one of those now. ⇩

_____

_____

_____

_____

_____

_____

_____

_____

Now, write down how that would play out in a perfect relationship:

_____

_____

_____

Now, consider making up a good, positive reason or lesson as to why that event might have happened.

What lesson came from that event? Or, what did you gain?

_____
_____
_____

What did you lose from it?

_____
_____
_____

How can you get back what you lost?

_____
_____
_____

What will you do differently if that comes up again?

_____
_____
_____

See what you just did there? You just broke down the facts about a turning point in your relationship and came up with an alternative plan in case it ever happens again. You're putting the focus on yourself and seeing the situation as something to grow from.

"It is not the stress that kills us, it is our reactions."

\-   Hans Selye

Chapter 4:
Your Brain and Physical Health

Our brains high on unhealthy relationships can cause physical health problems later on, if not already.

Dr. Will Cole, a functional medicine expert, specializes in clinical research about a plethora of health problems from brain issues, to hormonal imbalances, to specific body organ conditions. Throughout his 12-year longitudinal study where he followed and interviewed approximately 10,000 people for 12 years, he discovered that the stressors experienced in toxic relationships and physical health is a real, true concern.

From that study, it was found that those who were in toxic relationships had greater chances of developing heart issues such as a heart attack or stroke. Think back to when you might have been stressed from an argument or from frequent arguments; your heart rate and blood pressure were likely elevated. Toward the end of my marriage, I noticed my smart watch would let me know when my heart rate was too high for too long during times when I was worried about a confrontation from the ex. Maybe you get headaches regularly because you're constantly on your phone avoiding your partner and maybe looking up relationship advice, and you suffer from potentially debilitating symptoms that could have been avoided. Maybe you don't sleep as well as you used to, either from the partner snoring, animosity, or feeling like you're lacking the connection that you wish you had. All of this over a long time span can cause major damage in the long run.

This area of knowledge presents an opportunity that will be conveyed in the Love Yourself section coming up. You'll learn how to connect your mind and body response to both stress and joy.

Additionally, long term stress from relationshits can lead to adrenal fatigue which is a non-specific condition that is associated with problems such as: sleep disturbances, fatigue, body aches, and chronic inflammation problems. The adrenal glands in our bodies produce cortisol, the "stress hormone", which if it produces more cortisol than the average non-stressed person, that abundance can cause internal exhaustion. Have you found yourself more worried about your health at all since the start of the relationship? This is something that I HIGHLY encourage you to put your pride aside and consider.

Now for some self-reflection.

What do you do to cope with relationship stress?

_____

_____

What do you do for mental stimulation at home?

_____

_____

What or who is your outlet to help you let out your emotions?

_____

_____

When it comes to learning to love yourself, or have self-compassion, learning about your body's natural responses may help you learn to change your focus in the moment of distress to help your body.

For example, when my ex would be on his way home and I was worried if he would say something awful about the dinner I was cooking, or call me a fuck*ng slob over a little dust bunny under the cabinet, or whatever he would feel like getting under my skin about - I would feel my heart race, thud, and skip. I'd feel like I'm choking a little bit, and he wasn't even home yet. Of course, my situation was very different than yours might have been, but the overall idea is that when I would feel anxious about my so-called partner, I would feel it in my body almost to the cellular level.

When I bought my smart watch, I started to track my heart rate. I noticed that every evening before he would get home, my heart rate would be between 100-120, which is too high for comfort because I was not running a mile: I was just living. I then started focusing on closing my eyes and slowing my breaths while telling myself, "Right now, you are okay. When he's home, you still will be okay. Your son is okay, you can breathe" among other affirmations that would bring me to that moment in time, bringing down my heart rate, and allowing me to think clearly.

Chapter 5:
Compassion and Beliefs

Self-compassion
Goal-setting
Getting Out

In order to make sure that whatever decision you're about to make will be a healthy one, it is absolutely crucial that you clear your head, clear your conscious, and stabilize your emotions. A bitter mind will cause bitter words which will create a whole different, bitter conflict.

In this chapter you will learn some simple tools to help you purge your life and your mind... remember, the most important part of this process is to have **empathy** and **compassion**. Not just for yourself, but for your partner and kid(s) - if you have them - as well.

#1: Love Yourself
Be compassionate to yourself, KNOW yourself.

You may have been fighting for this relationship because you love your partner... or believe that you do. You might be afraid of hurting your partner, and that's okay. That just means you're a kind person. But let me ask you this. Are you just as kind if not more to yourself as well?

At this point in time, it is important to think of yourself. Give yourself the compassion that you deserve without seeking it from another person. You are the boss of your brain and the healer of your heart. You are the only one who can savor your senses - no one else. Forcing these thoughts to stay in your forefront of your mind may help you see that you have not been embracing these wonderful parts of your personality and soul. You may feel finally allowed to open your mind to more possibilities of personal development and get to know your body's response to any given situation.

To guide you through this, I will walk you through two exercises.

First, write down two physical responses you notice in your body when you think about your current relationshit status. How are you breathing? Are you jittery? Do you feel any rise in blood pressure or heart rate? Does anything twitch? If not, think of something that stresses you out about your relationshit.

1. When I think of:

    I feel this in my body:

2. When I think of:

    I feel this in my body:

This is not an easy exercise and it might take some time for you to realize your body's responses. That's okay. Just keep this in mind for your health's sake. Knowing where in your body your tension arises will bring mindfulness to your emotions, and allow you to recognize, acknowledge, and nurture them.

Next, write down 5 things that you absolutely love about yourself... it could be personality traits, skills, literally anything. **These are parts of you that you will not let anything in this world change or destroy.**

1.

2.

3.

4.

5.

Amazing job! Now here's the tricky part... Read each statement again, followed by the following phrase:
"This is me. No one can change that. I can finally fully embrace this part of me without (partner's name)."
Say this as many times as it takes for it to become engraved in your mind.

Now, cross out any of those that you feel may be hindered or pushed under a rug by your relationship. Do you get to openly, naturally allow those traits to show on a daily basis without fear or shame?

If you find that some of your traits are hidden because of a reason related to the relationship, then think to yourself about what you can do to get those back and be your true self.

This part may be difficult for many people, I know it was for me. It literally took me about a week just to fill all of these 5 traits in. Once I finally did, I realized that over half of these traits I loved about myself were pieces of my soul that were lost for so long while I was surviving my relationshit. Now that I was able to fill my own tank with the affirmations I have always craved, I was able to be more kind to myself. My self-esteem and confidence was crushed and I didn't even realize it, then I had a therapist give me a more in-depth version of what you just did.

It is possible that you might be wondering why we are not listing out what you love about your partner. I hate to break it to you, but we are here to focus on you. We will touch on what you like about your partner later.

#2: Make Brief, Realistic Goals, Not vague, sh*tty ones.

Making brief and realistic goals can help keep you focused on your mission to freedom. The goals give you your own set of boundaries, rules, and guidance through a major hurdle you are about jump over. Making realistic goals keeps us accountable and gives us a higher chance at preventing us from changing our minds or taking different routes that might lead to danger.

For this next part, write down 3 things that you will work toward regarding your breakup/divorce. They should be Specific, Measurable, Attainable, Realistic, and Timely.
    (example: I will partake in one self care activity for one hour everyday until the divorce). (another: I will read the rest of this book by Friday night.)

1.

2.

3.

For all we know, your partner may be thinking the same thing you are and is just waiting on you to make the move. You are the bigger person. The fact that you're reading this right now shows and proves that you are ready to step out of your comfort zone and start your life over and thrive. Woohoo!! Go you!!

#3. Literally get out.
Get out of your environment, get out of your HEAD.

Get out of your **Environment and into a new one.**

Some say being out in nature is better than Prozac (an antidepressant if you didn't know). Others might not feel peace in nature at first because it is out of their comfort zone. If you are "Some" and love being in nature, then make it happen as soon as possible. If you're in the kind of situation where maybe you don't have a vehicle, or are bogged down by your job, this might be the time to use a sick day and to sweet talk a good friend into letting you borrow a car or go out for a long walk or bike ride. Find a way to make it happen and stop making excuses. Even take a Greyhound bus or train somewhere. Then, Use this to-do list as a guide:

1. Pick somewhere that you love or that you want to check out.

2. Get in touch with your closest friends and family members and tell them that your phone will be on airplane mode for a couple of days

and about where you'll be heading... invite your favorite person if you want. That way of course if something happens they'll know where to look for you.

3. Make a playlist/mixtape with only songs with positive messages. If they talk about how much life sucks, then that kind of defeats the purpose. I had a "Happy Songs only" playlist and it pumped me up!

4. If you're driving, take the scenic route. Stop and take pictures on the side of the road or maybe hike down the side of the freeway to a hidden river... Shoot, I once drove down the Pacific Coast Highway and pulled over and climbed down this rocky pathway. I ended up just taking a catnap and even rubbed one out under this random bridge by the ocean. I was actually pretty scared, wondering "what if someone walks up on me or tries to be a dick?"...but I was in a 'fuck it' kind of mood and there wasn't a soul in sight. It was liberating.

If you're taking a greyhound or train, get off at random stops and explore random little towns. Treat yourself to a local pub, food joint, music venue, whatever sounds good! Then catch the next train towards your destination. Of course, if the area doesn't feel safe, just keep on riding and don't go there.

If you're just taking a walk/hike in your local area, stop and take pictures of little critters, plants, or whatever catches your eye. Look at the details in your surroundings and see what you can find.

5. Wherever you end up, focus on your breathing. Smell the air of where you are and absorb it like a medicinal inhaler. If it smells like the urine of the crowded streets of a college town, then I understand if you choose to not indulge in this practice.

6. Live on the land. Take a tent and some camping stuff, or even sleep in your car. Take some food, maybe some MRE's from Amazon or a bunch of non-perishable snacks. This kind of helps you realize in a subtle way that you have a lot to be thankful for.

7. Whatever you do, DO NOT CONTACT YOUR PARTNER. Seriously. JUST DON'T. This is YOU time. If you do, all of this will be for nothing. If you succumb, then it's crucial that you try again another day when you feel strong enough to disengage from the partner for a day or two.

Let this excursion be your time to bring peace, quiet, and clarity to your mind. Don't talk about your partner. Don't contact your partner. Don't get drunk, because you'll lose control and probably think about your partner and make contact.

In January 2017, I was at the point in my marriage (we were together for 7 years total at this point) where I knew it was over and I wanted to leave, but was just waiting for the right time. I was tired of walking on eggshells, I was tired of being verbally attacked on a daily basis over the most insignificant things, and was tired of allowing him to make me feel worthless. So one morning I told him, "Hey, hold the baby for the weekend I'm going away. I'm heading to Tahoe but I don't know where exactly." As he started asking questions, I was already out the door. I knew he would do better as a dad without his triggering person around. You know, because my whole being was his trigger as he was mine.

I stopped at the grocery store and grabbed a bunch of beef jerky, trail mix, fruit etc. and drinks and just started driving. I didn't even use my map because I figured I could just follow signs towards Tahoe and see where I ended up.

While driving through the mountains, whenever I would approach a turnout I would pull over and see what's on the other side of the highway safety rail. There were a couple of times when there would be a trail leading down to a river so I would just climb down and go walk along the river and skip some rocks and relax... maybe even squat and void my bladder. Then I would just climb on back up to my car and keep on driving. When I got to South Lake Tahoe, I stopped and did a little gambling, lost 20 bucks - oh well it was fun - did a little gangster rap karaoke in front of some strangers who gave me at least 10 high-fives, and went to my room to read and relax in a tub.

I tried my best to stay in the mindset that I was alone, that I could do and say whatever I wanted without being judged, criticized, or ignored. With every bit of joy that I felt on this trip, I would tell myself that damn, I am enjoying this moment and no one is here to ruin it for me. I'm not going to worry about what it would be like if someone was here, because no one IS here. I HAD to stay in the moment and not imagine any "what if" situations because they just weren't realistic and damn it, they would sure ruin the mood. If I caught myself trying to think, "damn, I wish he and I could be doing this together like the old days", I would literally shake my head like an Etch-a-Sketch and say "Fu*k that, we'd be resenting each other, it'd be awkward, we'd just ignore each other anyways"... #mindfulness.

Now when you go embark on a random road trip somewhere nice, do whatever you want. If something pops in your head, just do it... don't worry about asking somebody's permission or trying to compromise with somebody. Just go do it. Don't be about it, don't let your good and evil conscience come into play, just do it.

Now of course this doesn't mean go do heroin or crack cocaine or kill somebody... I'm talking about activities that are not those things. Go do some random acts of kindness, go find something that will pump up your adrenaline, whatever will make you feel whole. If some crazy idea comes up, don't question it - just make it fucking happen.

On this trip, focus on you. Focus on each and every moment that you were experiencing. Every moment of joy, peace, and tranquility. Tell yourself over and over again that you will never feel this way with the person you're stuck with. Tell yourself that you love this moment, and if you feel like you don't want to be alone, remind yourself that there may be somebody better he would feel the same way and is tranquil and peaceful as you are. You love yourself, you are amazing, and don't let yourself forget it.

This is the trip where you need to remember all these things and you may need to even write on sticky notes, set reminders for yourself to remind yourself to think this way, whatever it may take. But think about being alone - not lonely.

The trip that I took wasn't anything extravagant nor expensive but the fact that I was alone with my thoughts and did what I wanted made it so when I returned back home I had a totally new mindset. My head was clear and my "fuck it" mentality stuck with me for a couple more months. When he would throw his verbal frying pans at me (so I called them), I actually for once had some quick, quirky comebacks that made me feel a smidge of victory! "What? What was that - that I just said?" I would ask myself literally out loud after he left the room. "Shit, I could get used to this!" I kept thinking to myself.

#4. Get Out of Your Head and Change Your Beliefs.

Get out of your OLD BELIEFS!

When we're faced with stressful situations, we may go into fight, flight, or freeze mode. When faced with a daily, repetitive, unfulfilling and unrewarding routine, we may go into stagnation - similar to hamsters who spin on wheels that never stop, or how birds fly against the wind and go nowhere. That's essentially being stuck in freeze mode because you're really not doing anything about it all.

Our beliefs and perceptions are the frontline actors of our minds. They act out and behave as we develop and maintain our beliefs and perceptions. Our beliefs can be outlined using the Health Belief Model, developed by social psychologists in the 1950s. In the Health Belief Model, we focus on:

1. Perceived **threats** - what we perceive as being personally threatening
2. Perceived **susceptibility** - how likely we believe we are at succumbing to a threat
3. Perceived **severity** - how severe we believe the damage could be
4. Perceived **barriers** to preventing such damage and our abilities to become self-sufficient in changing our ways for the better

The Health Belief Model

Source: DOI: 10.3109/14992027.2013.791030

In stagnant, low-quality relationships, we tend to **believe** that our **threat** is low. Perhaps what we have already been going through is "not so bad" or "could be worse" - yet we are still struggling to breathe fresh air. When we stay in such situations for long periods of time, we fall into a habit trap that we actually just get used to and tolerate. It becomes all that we know, similar to a drug addiction.

If you take action now and change your **beliefs**, realize that what you read about earlier and the potential health effects that you are likely to encounter sooner or later, you can change your current low **Threat Perception** into something more of a high concern.

For example:

If you found out that your shitty relationship is causing you to have as high of a chance of having a heart attack as a chronic two-pack-a-day cigarette smoker with high blood pressure, would you consider changing your beliefs (your perceived threat) about your relationship?

Now, say that you do not wish to change your beliefs still because you might die of a heart attack regardless if you're in the relationship or not. In that case, your current **perceived susceptibility** suggests that you believe that you are **susceptible** to the heart attack death no matter what you do - so now that **belief** poses a **barrier**. What needs to happen in order to break this barrier? Perhaps you could re-shape your beliefs to support the prevention of the threat.

Your susceptibility perception is that if you keep in your relationship, you may have a greater chance of having a heart attack, so make changes now. Your end of the relationship is in your control.

Your reality is a reflection of your strongest belief.

You may **believe** that your lifestyle is normal, expected, or that there is nothing you can do.

You may **believe** that you do not have the right to end a committed relationship.

You may **believe** that you are not entitled to your own personal space, clear boundaries, and/or freedom.

If you believe any of these thoughts or anything similar to such, it's time to figure out a new way of believing.

Chapter 6. Tabs and Action Plans
Keep Tabs on the Conflicts &
Make Plans for the Tabs

Do you feel that you can say what's on your mind without fear of upsetting the other person or letting yourself down? I hope that now your mind and thoughts are clear and ready to be put into a more new and improved use. Now is the time to keep a list or tabs on every reason why you should leave and why **you** should be the one to pull the plug.

Back to my solo-trip, when I returned from Tahoe I had this new way of thinking, communicating, and even breathing. Almost everything that would come out of my mouth towards my husband at the time was sarcastic and I took no offense to any of his verbally abusive comments where before I would normally go numb and fight myself in my head. I stopped taking everything personally, because on that trip I realized that I am not the problem.

Now your situation of course might be very different from mine, you might not have any kind of abuse or verbal frying pans being thrown at you at all... But you do have reasons to leave and that's why you should keep tabs on them.

No matter how small and insignificant something may be, you must tell yourself that you are not making any excuses for that little situation. Perhaps you could keep a little journal or keep notes in a notes app on your phone (password protected if necessary!) With whatever tool you decide upon, write down what happened and what you did in response to the event. Keep it factual and allow yourself to verbalize your emotions as you feel them - do not let them dictate the reality of the situation and cloud the facts. You're holding yourself accountable and showing both sides of the story.

Some examples:

Today, he/she ignored me when I tried to talk about what's for dinner. I ended up making dinner for myself. Normally I would be upset, but this time I felt at peace.

Today, he/she and I could not agree on who's picking up our child. I said I'd do it but had to switch my work around. I was frustrated, but I did not yell. I just made it happen.

Today, he/she complained of "xyz" and I didn't even care to listen.

Just now, she yelled at me for not texting her back right away. I ignored her and it felt so good.

It doesn't matter how severe or small the situations are. Once you have a decent list and you read through it all then you can actually see in black-and-white, in front of you, that this relationship will not be going any further. It can even be used as living proof to show the other person when you have that conversation to break it off if you feel it would strengthen your case.

Action Plans

This is the part where you plan out this conversation, and you may base it on the tabs you have been keeping. The trigger pull, the thread pull, the bridge burn, the whatever-you-want to call it... this is the part where you are the bigger person, where you are the game changer, and where both of your lives are about to change, hopefully for the better. I want to help you walk through this process with the dignity that you know you have. You both have been living as roommates... Loveless lovers... two people who grew apart and are in either denial or stuck.

Being alone in a relationship is much worse than being alone and by yourself. It's like having a tortilla that you expect your partner to fill with the best ingredients and goodness where instead, you could make your own burrito how you want it... and eat it too.

Here is the step-by-step method of how I prepared for my relationshit's end:

1. If you are cohabitating, **find yourself a new place to live**. Take the initiative. Be the bigger person and remember that it is easier to control what you do versus what your partner will do.
- Go online
- Physically walk into apartment rental offices
- Drive to a realty office and talk to a realtor.
- **Make appointments to scope out a new place so you can hold yourself accountable as if you had a doctor's appointment.** (This is for your mental and physical health, afterall!)

The caveat: You must do this **alone** and without your partner knowing. Once you find something, schedule your moving date or schedule a meeting with a realtor.

Potential repercussions: You might end up scolded for doing all of this behind your partner's back. You might feel guilty, second-guess yourself, and have a hard time deciding because you keep wondering if the other person will like it. **Prove yourself wrong by remembering this:** **You are knocking down the walls of a toxic dump that has been overtaking the beauty and splendor of your life.**

2. If you're not married, skip to #3. If you are married, file for divorce. In my county, it was $435 to file. If you must, pull out a payday loan, personal loan, borrow, break into savings, get more hours at work if you need help paying for it. Go to the courthouse, and speak to a family law office to get you started. It will cost some money, a few hundred bucks in many counties... but it'll will be the ticket to a new, fresh start.

3. Think of a brief - but powerful - speech that you plan on saying to your partner. This should be less than 2 minutes because once someone's emotions set in, it will get out of control from there and go in one ear and out the other. Keeping it short, sweet, and straightforward is the key to your freedom.

Speech Tips:
1. Use facts that you wrote down from your Tab keeping.
2. Use those "I" statements that you've learned about in your attempts to fix things.. Write the speech, end it with a final word, and think about walking away as soon as you finish. Practice it in your head. Have a close friend review it for you if you must.

Take out a piece of paper and a pen. List out numbers 1-10, and write a step-by-step action plan on how you are literally going to initiate this break. It may help you keep accountable and remember where you are when you're going through a difficult and stressful time. I made mine the morning that I realized I needed to go to the courthouse.

Here is what my divorce plan looked like:

1. Go to courthouse, file for divorce.
2. Print out a description of the type of abuse that I endured to highlight why I am leaving to support the reasoning.
3. Print out a copy of a signed restraining order and attach a note saying that I will have it filed if he blows up my phone or threatens me in any way.
4. Find someone that I know is strong to have him served in case he blows up. Also figure out when he will be alone because I don't want to humiliate him in front of his coworkers.
5. Pack a bag for myself and my son in case he reacts violently.
6. Find somewhere else to stay, whether a friend's place, with family, or in a hotel. Give a specific time frame (one week for example) so you do not overstay your welcome and do not spend more hotel money than you need to.
7. Schedule the serving of papers, make sure your bag is in your car. Make sure you are in a public, safe location during that time.
8. Let him cool off. Do not engage in arguing or answering his questions, so turn your phone to airplane mode for the rest of the day.

9. When you turn your phone on again, analyze his messages from an empathetic perspective. This guy just got dumped or divorced after so many years of being together. His manhood must be crushed. He must feel like a failure or he must feel like his whole world just crumbled. Put your own emotions aside and know that you might have shocked him.

10. Simply ask him "is it safe to come back tonight or do I need to go elsewhere?" You are in control of where you go, you cannot control where he goes.

11. Plan for a follow-up conversation about child custody, selling the house, and anything else important.

I hope this section opened your mind to the logistical planning it took me to successfully end my marriage. You may tweak yours to your preference of course.

PART THREE.

What to F*cking do, Once and For all.

Chapter 7: The Physical Process

Split the breakup process into 3 major phases.

*** It is highly important to read through
all phases before commencing
the breakup/divorce.***

Phase 1 - Preparation

Make More Specific Goals.

Now that you know what you want, set some goals for planning the break-up. Again, make sure they are SMART: Specific, Measurable, Attainable, Relevant, and Time-bound.

Examples: I will physically go look at 3 rental homes for myself before Friday. Today, I will reserve an outdoor seating dinner for two at Olive Garden for Friday at 6pm. Today, I will write down my 3-minute break-up speech and call my good friend tonight at 5pm to give me feedback on it.

Now, make those goals! Let's start with 3.

1.
2.
3.

Go back, are they specific enough? Will you hold yourself accountable? Good! Set some alarms in your phone if you have to!

Set the Setting: *Time and place is* **crucial.**

When thinking of a place to physically end the relationshit, please follow these guidelines:

- ☒ This place has no special meaning to you two
- ☒ It is public but not crowded. Do not put your partner in a spotlight, but stay public for your safety.

- ☒ Schedule it as something they should prepare themselves for, like a doctors appointment.
- ☒ There should be space between you two, such as a table.
- ☒ No alcohol - this can cause words to be misused or misinterpreted and emotions to be stronger.

Communication: *Phone, text, or person?*

- ☒ **In-person** works well if you are confident enough to follow these 3 rules without even considering breaking them.
- ☒ **Video chat** works if you feel that there will be a violent or unmanageable reaction, and you can still follow these 3 rules.
- ☒ Letters, texts, voice messages, emails are all horrible, passive, and non-compassionate.

TIPS:

- ☒ Phrasing must be short and sweet and clear.
- ☒ Don't give false hope.
- ☒ Don't give examples, just keep it short and sweet. IF you feel examples are necessary, go back to those tabs you kept in the "Tabs and Action Plans" section.
- ☒ Use "I" or "we" instead of "you". Saying "You this" "You that" will cause the soon-to-be ex to get defensive and nothing productive will get done. You're talking about how you feel about the facts.

Contingency Plan: *Have an easy exit in case the reaction goes wrong*

- ☒ First, set clear boundaries
- ☒ Know when to leave

Once you have the date, time, and place in mind, schedule it with your partner. Let your partner know that you want to talk about something important to you. That's it. No need to elaborate.

You want to prepare the partner for a potentially long conversation. If he/she thinks it's a date and goes in expecting a good time, they will likely react harshly and impulsively and you won't be able to get your words through.

Let's take a peek at some ways to respond to some behaviors that you might encounter:

1. If you're asked "What's it about?" or "Why?", just breathe, check your posture and have confident body language, and say that you want to make sure you're on the same page with some things, and that you'll talk about the details later. Nothing more. Boundary set.

1. If you're asked, "Are you leaving me?" then that is an immediate red flag that shows how insecure your partner is. If they are that insecure to jump to that conclusion, then you have all the right in the world to **simply say "should I?"** and leave it at that. Say you will see him/her at dinner. If that is expected to happen, be sure to read Phase 2 before acting.

If your partner starts yelling, manipulating you, twisting your words, arguing - just walk away. Let that fireball cool off. Do not attempt to explain yourself at this point; it will not work. Go to the reserved dinner you planned anyway, and let it be a moment to absorb that conversation and enjoy some good food. Maybe your new maybe cooled-off ex will show up so you can talk, maybe not.

At that point, give it some time and see if the fireball did ever cool off enough to meet in person. If you need to go to your residence and get your things, bring someone strong with you.

2. You might be asked, "Is everything okay?". You can reply, "Not at the moment, but everything will be okay," - find a way to shed some light on a dark situation with a silver lining. That will also open up to change the expectations of your partner.

Take a moment to think about other responses you would feel confident in saying if you are asked the following questions when you set up the dinner date:

- Are you leaving me?
- Is everything okay?
- What's this about?
- What are we celebrating?

Phase 2 - The Break

Keep it brief, simple, and powerful.

Remember, this book is to help you end this shitshow respectfully and in a way that keeps you both on the same page.

My 3-step rule for the in-person, life-changing, nerve-wracking moment.

1. Keep eye contact

2. Focus the Conversation

3. Walk out when Emotions Start

1. <u>Keep solid eye contact.</u>

You're nervous. You're feeling the pressure. You're about to go into a Lion's cage to break some news that he won't be getting steak from now on, and if you break eye contact your life could be in jeopardy.

Moving your eyes back and forth or away may indicate a lack of confidence or dishonesty - both which could trigger the new ex to take advantage of and twist around. Practice in front of a mirror or a trusted friend. Take videos of yourself and watch it, if you feel it's necessary.

If you had the ex served with divorce papers, it may help to let this time be where you talk about the divorce and make sure that everything is going to be understood and that boundaries are set.

If you have nothing left to share with the ex (no kids, nothing of yours at the house) then let this moment be the most respectful, compassionate way you could possibly end this.

I made a dinner reservation the night that I had my ex served. At that dinner, I kept to these 3 rules and made sure that he understands my boundaries that I laid before him, and where we talked about plans for our son.

As soon as he started talking about suicidal ideations, I got up and went to the bathroom. I told myself that he is feeling down, depressed, and hopeless so I need to make sure to find a way to get him back to the topic and have some compassion.

We ended that night amicably, and he started changing his behaviors almost immediately to please me.
(I didn't fall for it, I kept my ground and reminded him that the divorce is still happening.)

2. <u>Keep the conversation focused.</u>

You are here for one thing: to end the shitty, stale, stagnant, unfulfilling, and un-relatable relatioshit that you have been stuck in for so long.

<u>Unmarried script - next page</u>

<u>Married script - page 113</u>

The unmarried script:

If you are **not married**, you are about to initiate this breakup. You are about to pull the trigger on some potential heavy emotions that you didn't know existed in your partner. If you are married and just served the divorce papers, the initial damage has already been done and you can skip to the next section "if you are married".

Back to you, you non-married badass person.

Keep this ad-lib script idea in your forethought
to help guide the conversation:

1.   Start with some **positives**. Even if it's hard to find
any these days, think of these as you picture this person
you're ending it with: what is your new ex good at? What
are they passionate about (even if it clearly is not you)?

2.   Share some **appreciation** for those aspects
alone. (Try to find some appreciation at least)

3.   State the **greatest lesson** you
have learned in one sentence.

4.   Simply state that **you are going to apply** that
lesson, and that it is important to share. Set a
boundary so you can finish before emotions fly.

5.   State that your application of that lesson
is to **end the relationship**. Use **"I" statements,**
because this is about you and your life only.

BREAKUP SCRIPT EXAMPLE:

1.   You are a: hard worker, charming, good cook, handy, dedicated to your (sport/ activity of choice), and are great at sex.

2.   I appreciate you for those, and I hope that you never change those about you.

3.   One lesson I have learned over the years is that we can't change anyone except ourselves.

4.   I am making some drastic changes and I feel it is important that I share these with you. They are hard for me to say so I ask that you please allow me to finish.

5.   I am unhappy with certain aspects of our life that I feel I cannot come back from. There are major parts of this life that affect my mental and physical health, and the only medicine that I feel would be the most effective is for me to end our relationship.

Now go to Step 3.

<u>The Newly Divorced Script</u>

If you are married, at this point you have already filed for divorce and had your partner served. Your partner may have or may not have had enough time to cool off and gather one's thoughts.

Remember that you still might be facing a fuming fireball of a person, so if you need to wait a day or so until you can have a conversation about the divorce, then do so. Just do not put it off too long, more than 3 days max.
Have the conversation before you start packing up the house so you do not leave your soon to be ex hanging.

Remember we are in this to end it with compassion, self-respect, and logic.

Here is a script that I followed the
night that I filed for divorce.

1. Start with some **empathy.** Your spouse was
just delivered the most potentially devastating
papers and you cannot expect this person to be
calm and happy. Share that feeling of shame. Set a
boundary so you can finish before emotions fly.

2. Share some **positives**. Even if it's hard to find any
these days, think of these as you picture this person
you're ending it with: what is your new ex good at? What
are they passionate about (even if it clearly is not you)?

3. Share some **appreciation** for those aspects
alone. (Try to find some appreciation at least)

4. State the **greatest lesson** you have learned
from marriage in one sentence. It is not necessary
to say that the lesson was from the marriage.

5. Simply state that **you are going to apply** that
lesson, and that it is important to share.

6. State that your application of that lesson is
to **end the relationship**. Use **"I" statements,**
because this is about you and your life at this
point, because that's what you can control.

DIVORCE SCRIPT EXAMPLE:

1. Empathy: I can't imagine the pain you must feel after receiving the papers. I would like to be on the same page with you so that way it takes the edge off of both of us.

2. Positives: I want you to know that I appreciate the things you do for me, working on my car, taking care of our kid, helping pay bills. You're a talented mechanic, a loving father, and a hard-worker.

3. I appreciate you for those.

4. The greatest lesson that I have learned from our marriage is that I cannot control or change anyone except myself. It was a hard lesson, probably the hardest lesson ever.

5. I'm applying that lesson by filing for this divorce and I truly want this to be the most civil, respectful process for the sake of our son and for our mental health.

6. So from this point on, I will be moved out by the end of this week. We will need to schedule a meeting to talk about child custody. I am not changing my mind, and I hope that we both become better people from our time apart.

Remember: Thes scripts are not long at all. It must be short, sweet, and to-the-point. No tangents, no stories, just raw information.

3. Walk out when emotions arise.

At this point, whether it's your emotions or your new ex's emotions, you both become vulnerable. When you're vulnerable, you might make a decision that you'll regret.

Right now, you are a professional. You are emotionally detached. Save your vulnerable moments for when you're safe and in a comfortable space so you can nurture and meditate on them.

If you need to cry, let off steam, or explode - Get up and walk out. Just leave. If your new ex starts saying things to get you to a vulnerable state - remember what triggers you, and get out before you become triggered.

If your new ex starts shouting at you, cussing at you, or behaves in a disrespectful way - get up and get out. If the food is still coming, forget about the food. Just go.

Phase 3 - Rehabilitation and Recovery

Congratulations! You just did one of the absolute most difficult tasks of mankind. You may be flooded with emotions, thoughts, and questions at this moment, but before we go into the emotional process, allow me to guide you through a few self-care activities first.

First, AVOID THESE TRAPS:

Alcohol
Alcohol can become excessive because it is likely to cause uncontrollable emotions and behavior. It is a depressant class of drugs, and the last thing you need is depression. Even one glass of wine can set off a downward spiral.

Social Media
You may have the urge to see what he/she is posting about the breakup, which can trigger you to react in ways that you might regret, and you might see things that will make you lose sleep. Log out of all social media for at least a few days while you get your head clear.

Romantic Movies and Songs
As we talked about in the beginning, romantic movies and songs portray a false picture of how relationships work. You can easily get stuck in the "Coulda, woulda, shoulda" trap and live vicariously through such movies and songs. Be in the moment right now.

Online Dating

Setting up an online dating profile can be detrimental because you may subconsciously look for someone to fill in the gaps that your new ex did not fill for you. You might go on dates and catch yourself talking about your ex, your breakup, and to be honest - no one wants to hear that on a date. Mature people in the dating world are not looking for the rebound.

Take time off from dating, be with friends, be with family, go out and find a mindful activity to do such as martial arts or any kind of art. Free your mind from negative people. Read some self help books, binge watch YouTube videos on post-relationship recovery, or find a goal to actively work on.

Overall, it is absolutely essential that you take care of your emotional center in your mind. Emotions can trigger unhealthy behaviors and thoughts... which can lead you into traps that are extremely difficult to escape. Self-care is mandatory.

True love is unconditional.
Relationships are not.

- Grant Gudmunson

Chapter 8: Emotional Rehabilitation
*Using logic to help dig through
the muck of your emotions*

Using logic in a time of vulnerability such as this can be controversial. From my experience, sometimes logic is the first line of defense when against experiencing a fight-flight-freeze response. Logic can help slow our sympathetic nervous system - which also quickens heart rates, raises blood pressure, etc. It's where you think your way through a new environment that we need to adapt to. However, using logic does not... and I repeat DOES NOT mean overthinking. Using logic in this sense is where you find a balance between your emotions and your information processing. How will you process such emotions and make sure it's a healthy method? How can you avoid past mistakes, unhealthy behaviors, and navigate your limbic system with this roadmap that you've worked so hard to figure out? Now that's the kind of logic we're talking about.

Following a life-altering event such as a breakup/divorce, you may feel flooded with second-guesses, doubt, worry, shame, guilt, among countless other emotions.

Some internal challenges you may face include, but are not limited to:
- Regret
- Change of mind
- Reflection
- Need for jumping into another relationship
- Avoiding unhealthy mind-fuck behaviors

With this process, you should anticipate some intense, maybe new emotions. You may encounter the emotion of devastation, regret, guilt, depression, anxiety, among many others. Getting over the emotional process is not something that one can just sleep off or wait to pass; it requires effort.

For me, I was anxious about the idea of being alone for I had never lived physically alone before. I moved into my ex husband's apartment when I was 19 in 2009 and had been with him until 2017. Throughout the relationship I had long bouts of depression with feeling completely disconnected with everyone around me, and felt guilty as if I had failed as a woman.

They say "time will heal all wounds" but that is actually far from the truth. Time itself does not heal, and this is a highly common misconception.

This famous Ted Talk by Psychologist Dr. Antonio Pascuale-Leone encompasses the concept of getting over a relationship after it has ended and helped me see my situation in a different, more realistic light. What you might be feeling is the need to fulfil unfinished business.

You may find the Ted Talk here: https://www. youtube.com/watch?v=W6BYAjhjt38 or look up "Ted Talk How to Get Over The End of a Relationship by Dr. Antonio Pascuale-Leone".

Some of the key points that he makes in his speech opened my mind to the healing process and helped me get over it sooner than I imagined.

Allow me to walk you through the lessons I learned from that Ted Talk regarding the concept of blaming.

1. If you avoid issues or the person, nothing will change. What are you hoping to avoid?

   _____

   _____

2. Don't get stuck on blaming, but turn your focus on giving words to your feelings. What do you want to blame on your new ex?

   _____

   _____

3. Now turn those blames into feelings. Write in the simplest way that you can about how those blamed behaviors make you feel. For example "When my partner does not follow our budget, it makes me feel like we can't cooperate with one another.

   _____

   _____

4. When you feel emotional pain, slow down. Where is your pain? What specifically hurts? (that was rhetorical)

5. What do you NEED the most right now?

   _____

   _____

The best piece of advice about post-relationship life that I have seen from both men and women, is to date, marry, and get to fall in love with yourself...

not in a narcissistic way, but know what triggers you. Know what sparks inspiration. Know what butters your biscuits. Know what all makes your heart race, slow down, and skip.

If you have goals and aspirations, do them. Once you do, you'll fall in love with the fact that you are creating the life you want. I am a firm believer that life is not about finding ourselves, it's about creating ourselves. If you believe that your higher power is the one shaping and creating you, then look for those sly signs and understand the wise "why's" behind everything that happens in your life.

Give yourself the credit, admiration, and encouragement that you deserve and may have always wanted. Give a damn about yourself for once.

Lose that weight.
Clear your head.
Start that band.
Accomplish your goals.
Get that degree.
Write that book.

You've been held back for so long, and now you can finally give yourself what you need.

Chapter 9: Hope for the Future

How to keep your hope real and alive with my Top Two Tools

It is easy to kick yourself for having just lost a partner, yet the easiest (and I swear it's easier than you might think) is to simply change the words you use to describe your feelings and experiences about it.

You did not just lose a partner, you **gained** a stronger relationship with yourself. You **gained** freedom to do what you love and live a higher quality of life.

Now is the chance to reflect about your behaviors throughout the relationship and point out those that are areas to work on. Be careful to not kick yourself here though, this lesson you're about to teach yourself by reflecting is where your new seed of growth will be implanted in your mind.

Here you will learn how to nip old behaviors and beliefs that you might repeat later on.

1. The Thinking Traps exercise in chapter 2 will help you with this process in finding alternative ways of thinking and doing in more healthy and compassionate means. You can Google search "The Unhealthy Thinking Traps" and you will find visual infographics that you can print and fill out. You can download the app called Youper, which is my absolute favorite therapy app that walks you through thinking traps when you are feeling a negative emotion.

2. The most important job that you have from here on out, is to gain EMPOWERMENT through BOUNDARY-SETTING.

The Book <u>Boundaries in Dating</u> by

Dr. Henry Cloud and Dr. John Townsend is a truly amazing guide to help you with this new lifestyle. The book delves into the details of how setting boundaries defines and protects the most important parts of your being. Your ability to connect and trust others, your need to feel and own up to your feelings, your personal values, your behaviors, and your opinions and perceptions about yourself and the dating scene.

The thought of setting boundaries, at least for me, was and continues to be a daunting, intimidating concept. *How do you set them? What do you say? Will I offend the other person?*

Some examples of boundary-setting can include you telling future partners (and yourself):

- I am a sensitive person and can take offense to things easily, so I ask that you not say (these specific) kind of jokes.

- I am an introvert and need to have Friday nights to myself to unwind from the week.

- I have a child and his needs will always come first.

- I do not like talking about sex until I'm ready to initiate the conversation.

These tell your future partners, friends, lovers about your needs, your values, and your priorities. If they choose not to respect them, then see that as a big red flag and let them go before you get in too deep. Your values, needs, and priorities are what make you YOU in this point in your life. If any of those become sacrificed for your partner, then you lose a part of yourself and that is never good for anyone.

Now it's your turn to set some boundaries for yourself, for future dates, and even for friends and family. Write down the first things that come to mind. This is the last exercise I would like to see you partake in. Let's do a practice one first:

I do not like _____, so I ask that you please do not _____.

Now try to make 4 more different boundaries:

1. _____
2. _____
3. _____
4. _____

Now that you have an idea of some boundaries that you will set, it will be so much easier to weed out those who might lead you to poor relationships again in the future.

Earlier when you read about the myths that the media and movies convey, such as that Happy Ever After is easily achieved, or that the Honeymoon feeling lasts forever, those may still be subconscious thoughts that can jump to the front of your mind when you encounter someone exciting. Taking the time to learn about yourself and embrace your physical responses to everything that happens will be one of the greatest tools for your responses to future potential partners.

Once you learn how to recognize, acknowledge, and focus on your heart skipping beats when you meet someone who gives you that butterfly feeling, it may be easier to do the Thinking Trap exercise, and check your beliefs, parental experience repetition, and Media Myth traps. Doing these gives you the logical control over the emotion center in your own brain, giving you the empowerment to embrace your full self to the cellular level. It's hard. It is far from easy... but, it is essential, necessary, and will change your life forever.

I hope that this memoir and guide helps save your life from stagnation and unfulfillment and that you take these lessons to heart. You are NOT alone in this world, and never will be. Be well, and be good to yourself. Thank you so much for reading.

References

Beattie, M. (1986). Codependent No More.

Cole, W. (2016). Toxic Relationships Affect Health. Retrieved from: https://drwillcole.com/toxic-relationships-affect-health-according-science

Flaxington, B. (2017). You Can't Make Someone "Care". Psychology Today. Retreived from https://www.psychologytoday.com/us/blog/understand-other-people/201711/you-can-t-make-someone-care?amp

LaMorte, W. (2019). The Health Belief Model. Boston University School of Public Health

The Cognitive Exercises throughout this book are courtesy of the best tips and tricks that I learned through many years of family and individual psychotherapy.

Malkin, C. (2016). Four Keys to Leaving a Bad Relationship. Psychology Today.

AA.org. (1981). The 12 Steps of Alcoholics Anonymous. Alcoholics Anonymous Publishing.

CPSIA information can be obtained
at www.ICGtesting.com
Printed in the USA
FSHW011708250121
77853FS

9 781646 203369